Teamwork: Recipe to Your Business Success

"Don't Let Your Competition Get the Jump on Your Productivity, Creativity and Innovation"

by Jim Connolly
www.ceochef.com

Disclaimer

The purpose of this book is to educate and entertain. The author of the publisher does not guarantee that anyone following the ideas, tips, suggestions, techniques or strategies will become successful. The author and publisher shall have neither liability nor responsibility to anyone with respect to any loss or damage caused, or alleged to be caused, directly or indirectly by the information contained in this book

Get my personal help - See page 100 for details!

Table of Contents

Get my personal help - See page 100 for details!

Acknowledgments

Thank you to all the teams that we've worked with over the years. Your "playing full out" participation helped not only you, but us too. We learned right along with you what it takes to be a high functioning team that meet the needs of an ever-changing world economy.

Thank you to all of the organizations that we've helped. Your enthusiasm and feedback has provided us with valuable insight and observations that make up much of the content within this book.

For all of the great chefs, especially Gus and Emile, that have influenced me and taught me what it means to be an effective leader with my own teams.

And last, but certainly not least, to my "home team", friends and family, the original team that fuels and inspires me to reach beyond what I think is possible. Thank you Renee, my beloved wife, Christopher my son and "the kids".

About the Author

Jim Connolly - "America's Top Team Building Chef"

An unstoppable attitude and belief that every team has the ability to overcome any obstacle, Jim Connolly has helped transform over 50,000 people into dynamic, cohesive, action oriented team members.

Chef Jim has created one of a kind team building programs and keynotes speeches that touch the hearts and stomachs of some of America's top companies, which is why he's been called, "America's Top Team Building Chef!"

His cooking team building programs are the only one of its kind that is designed by a world class, celebrity Chef who is also an experienced corporate trainer.

Chef Jim was prompted to write this book because there is so much confusion to what makes up a world class team and how to keep your team focused on performing as a high functioning collective group. So you are not in the dark anymore, Jim has chosen to reveal that to you now - so you too can reap the rewards of a great team too!

www.ceochef.com
Tel: 888-308-TEAM

Get my personal help - See page 100 for details!

Introduction:

You can't blame us, it's not our fault!

We've been trained from all through our scholastic careers to be the best as an individual. Our motivation is as an individual, our assignments are mostly individual, and our grades are as individuals. It's no wonder that when we start to work in the real world, they ask us to work together as a team to maximize our results and we scoff at the idea, make a half-hearted attempt or just don't know how to do this!

I'm not blaming the school systems, they have enough on their minds than have us blame them for one more thing. They on the most part, do a great job preparing us for the business world. So it's our duty to address the 500 pound gorilla in our work places, our businesses and even in some of our families.

WE DON'T KNOW HOW TO WORK IN TEAMS!

There, it said it. The straight forward truth to the matter is that we are not nearly as effective as we must be to compete in the world economy as we think we are. The funny thing about it is that we are fooling ourselves by all agreeing that we work in teams when in actuality all we are doing is talking the talk, we haven't yet walked the walk. What does that mean to you is that we are leaving opportunities on the table for other companies and organizations who have identified that their most valuable asset are their people and who have embraced a team philosophy. It means that your company will miss (or in some cases, already missed) the next new innovation or need in our society because your teams are conditioned to not rock the corporate boat and keep the status quo. It means that as a company, you're not growing nearly as much as you could be and we know, just like for individuals, if you're not growing, you're dying!

Sure, are their companies that are striving to incorporate a team based culture in the work place, absolutely yes. Companies like Amgen, Google, Starbucks and more, embrace this team philosophy and it shows in their results as a company.

But there are so many companies that still rule with the philosophy, "It's my way or the highway!" mentality and it shows in the lack of creativity, passion and innovation that comes from the staff and employees which carries over in every department and eventually becomes the "being" of the company or core identification and paradigm that everyone lives by. And your results are not anywhere near as impressive as they could be.

Now, take a deep breath! Go ahead; there is good news on the way.

The good news is that to change your company and team core identification is as quick as a heartbeat or a snap of the fingers! There that simple. The trick is to first get everyone to buy into this new core identification and the second is once you and your team has gone through your transformation, how do you keep it there?

That is what this book is about, transforming your company, your team, even your family to be the best that you can be, be the most creative and innovative you can be, and have fun doing it! Yes fun, our secret weapon to motivate, educate and implement new ideas of being as a team. Our process is TAC™ or Team Associative Conditioning™, which is a fancy way of saying that we take any team, scramble their paradigm or belief of who they are and imprint over them a new blueprint of being that builds relationships, empowers creativity and innovation and overall changes the course of your organization forever!

Chapter One:

Why Build a Highly Effective Functioning Team?

Chapter One:

Why Build a Highly Effective, High Functioning Team?

When Jones died, he descended to hell, where he saw souls seated before a banquet of unimaginable bounty. However, a long spoon was strapped to each person's wrist, so long that he or she was unable to bring the delicacies to his or her own mouth.
And so everyone was full of frustration and rage.
In heaven, Jones found the same setup, except that everyone was radiantly happy.
For the people were using the long spoons to feed each other.

To be prepared to compete in a world economy you must have high performing, effective teams to take your company there! And today, we are all a part of a world economy. Even if all you do is sell product on EBay, you're selling your Aunt May's tea set to someone half way to Australia. You're in a world economy whether you planned on it or not. And the only way you can achieve the visions for your organization is by activating the most powerful asset at your disposal, the people in your teams

Don't believe me. In fact I'd like you to scrutinize everything that is said in this book so when you are ready, you become the biggest fan of teams out there.

Get my personal help - See page 100 for details!

I wasn't always a fan of building teams, it became something that I learned to love, appreciate and depend on. I started off like most people, going to elementary school with a goal to be the best student possible. Why, because my brother was a top student and I saw the attention that he got for from his academic success. So my early conditioning told me, just like it told many of us, that if we do well in school, we'll get rewarded. And of course the rewards came from our parents and teachers who stressed that the point for working hard was to eventually prepare us for a good job later, which would allow us to do the things that adults do, get married, have a home, a family and basically have what we have popularized as the "American Dream". All from doing well individually at school (a lot for a six year old to comprehend don't you think?)

Never did it say, work hard as a "team" and you'll get all of these things in the future. No, it said you work hard and you'll have it all.

It wasn't until junior high when I began to play organized sports that I had my first taste of what teamwork and the advantages it provided. In fact, I was like a "team" sponge at that point and played only sports that emphasized the team game. I was hooked. I would even play challenge court on the playgrounds with a basketball team formed from less than stellar skilled players because I knew that we could compete and beat those playground all-stars if we aligned ourselves together as a team.

As much as I got this message of the effectiveness of a high performing team, I never really connected the dots once I got to the working world. Like most people, I was ill-equipped to function within a team concept because of my conditioning was to function as an individual. My original degree and training was in Hospitality Management and Culinary Arts and I thought I was God's gift to the world of food and dining!

I'm told that it was my reptilian section of my brain that focused on survival, and that it was working overtime in the workplace, and that caused me to be so self-centered and cocky as a young up-coming apprentice chef. I think it was my ego running amuck pure and simple.

But nothing like a large dose of humility to turn my cocky ways around. It was when I met my mentor, Gus, that I started my journey to understand the meaning and power of being in teams.

Basically, Gus broke me like a wild stallion. First he put me in my place by out-working me, out-skilling me and out-thinking me in every area of the kitchen. Now, looking back, he didn't do that to show me how good he was and express his cockiness, but rather, he did it to show me of my "individual" limitations of trying to always go it alone.

Then he introduced to me the concept of working as a team on the hot line in the kitchen. Up until then, I would work my food station and didn't care about if the other cooks on

Get my personal help - See page 100 for details!

the line and if they were ready or not to put up their finished dishes, I'd send my food out first and expected them to meet my challenge of matching my speed and skill level.

Gus taught me, that the secret to his success as a high-end restaurant owner and chef, was looking at every night's service as a symphony and his responsibility was as the conductor of the symphony of dining. He explained that everyone had to play their part well and be in connection with the rest of the restaurant team. The way I was "being", a self-centered show-off, would be like the percussion section striking their drums twice as loud as needed, increasing the tempo of the music and basically creating chaos and ultimately, bad music. Gus's point became a part of me and it was reflected in my behavior while working for him.

Even though I eventually left my position with Gus, those lessons of team never left me. I devoted my life to the understanding of how to form the best teams possible. I applied Gus's principles everywhere I went until I settled in for 17 years at one of Silicon Valley's top restaurants. This is where I was free to apply Gus's high performance team principles to an already successful organization. The results were phenomenal! Four star ratings in all of the major Bay Area newspapers and magazines rated within the top five in food in all of the San Francisco Bay area according to the Zagat guide and generally considered a top rated destination restaurant experience. I say this not to impress you but to impress upon you that it wasn't me who made this happen;

Get my personal help - See page 100 for details!

it was our restaurant team that made us a success. Both the dining room staff and the kitchen staff would work in unison, as Gus's team principles had taught me, like a beautiful sounding symphony of food and service.

Now as wonderful as that sounds, and as tempting as it was to take all of the credit, my lessons with Gus reminded me of my own personal limitations and that the true power that I would weld was within a team structure as the leader of this team.

To keep me connected with this message, I continued my journey to be the best team leader I could be for my teammates by learning about human behavior, team dynamics, and organizational development from some of the masters like Tony Robbins, Michael Grinder, Ron Cole and many more.

I absorbed so much and applied it so well, that my team outgrew me and performed like rock stars without me. This was the sign that it was time to move on with a different purpose in mind.

So that was back in the early 90's when, what is now CEO Chef was conceived. Our purpose, through our unique processes, transform people into high functioning teams that bring creativity, productivity and achievement to companies and organizations. We accomplish this through our speaking, workshops and coaching.

Get my personal help - See page 100 for details!

So getting back to the question, why do you want to build highly effective teams within your business and organization? I think the question should be, why would you not constantly develop highly effective teams within your business and organization. There is no downside to this equation. One plus one now equals three! The meaning of synergy where the results are greater than the sum of your parts is experienced and you reap the benefits. Whether you are the head of a Fortune 100 cooperation, a small business, a non-profit organization or an entrepreneur, the concept is the same, building effective teams around you, maximizes production, which generates more revenue, reduces the outrageous cost of turnover and emphasizes employee engagement. All it takes is the commitment to team to make this possible. In many organizations and companies, a commitment has already been developed to leadership, individual testing, sales training, market research, and all individual development activities. It's now time to take all of that great individual development and connect the dots and apply it to developing your team(s).

Nothing is stronger or more powerful than a team with a singular vision and focus.

Individual commitment to a group effort, that is what makes a team work, a company work, a society work, a civilization work.
-Vince Lombardi

Chapter Two:

The Six Characteristics of a High Functioning Team.

Get my personal help - See page 100 for details!

Chapter Two:

The Six Characteristics of a High Functioning Team.

None of us is as smart as all of us.
-Ken Blanchard

During the 90's there was a show on television called "Herman's Head". It didn't spark a lot of critical acclaim and didn't last more than two seasons but its basic premise was that every person has a team within them, pulling the puppet strings that make our decisions depending on the circumstances. What was interesting was that this show illustrated the different characteristics that make up our personalities and these different personalities were influenced by their experiences.

Well teams are made up of different characteristics too. And they too are influenced by experiences. What make these team characteristics so important is that when they are working together, they create a sort of synergy that makes their results greater than the sum of their parts. In other words, a high powered, highly effective world class team!

The interesting thing about these team characteristics is that if you give them a value or rating that corresponds to the length of the spokes of a wheel, you have to ask yourself, how smooth is my ride? If all of the spokes are near equal length or value, then you <u>have the ability to move quickly and cover more terrain while enjoying a smooth ride</u> along the way. If your team characteristic spokes are inconsistent in length and value, how far and how quickly can you go?

Six Team Characteristics

1. Communication
2. Collaboration
3. Cooperation
4. Commitment
5. Trust
6. Leadership

A High Powered, Highly Effective World Class Team!

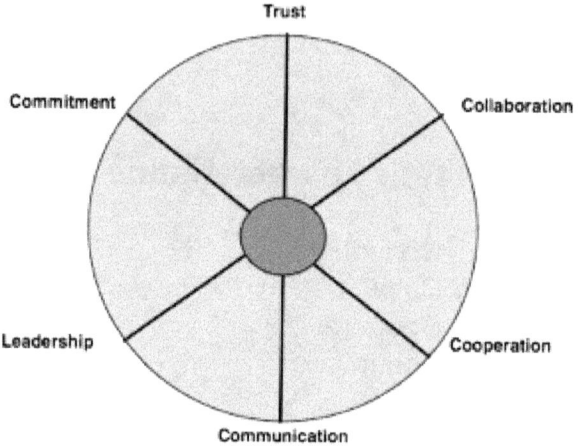

NOT

A High Powered, Highly Effective World Class Team!

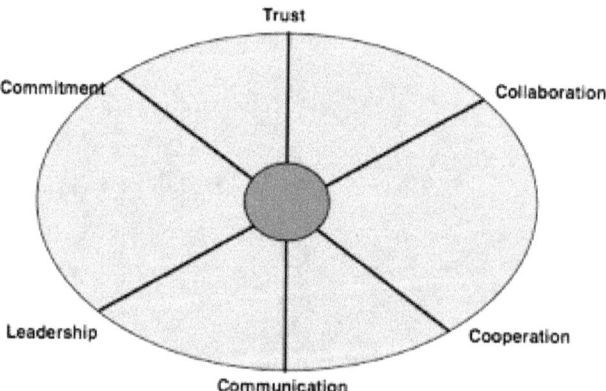

Bumpy Ride Ahead!

Rate Your Team!

Remember, this is to see your team's starting point. Where you stand right now as a collective group.
Oh, and if you're the designated leader of your team, remember, you're a part of your team too! So leadership should include you and the rest of your team.

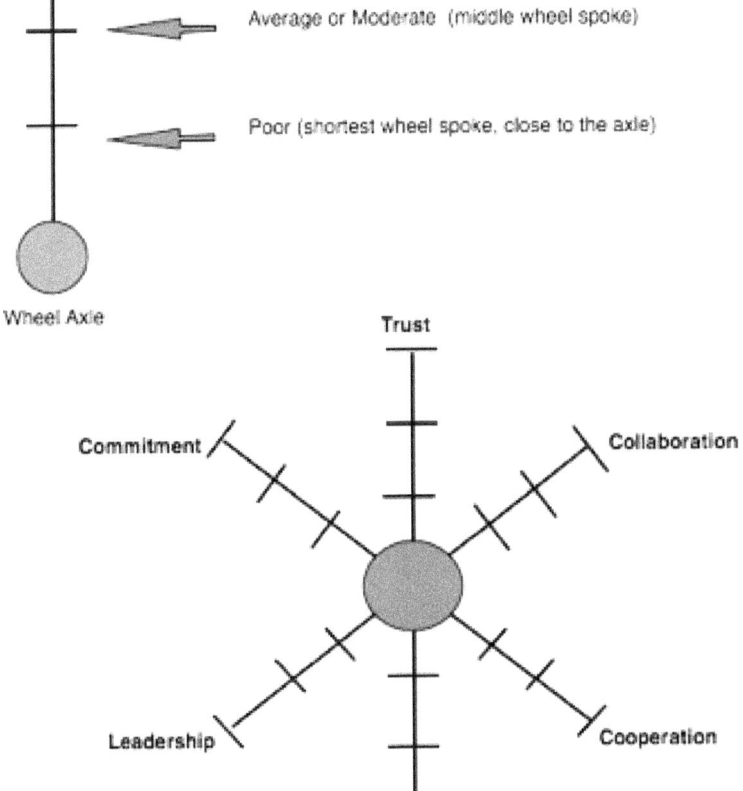

Outstanding in every way (longest wheel spoke)

Average or Moderate (middle wheel spoke)

Poor (shortest wheel spoke, close to the axle)

Wheel Axle

Connect the Points Where You Have Rated Your Team to Form Your Team Wheel.

Rate Your Team!

What Did You Learn?

How easy was it to rate you and your team in this exercise?

What team characteristics do you and your team rate outstanding or highly?

What team characteristics do you and your team rate moderate?

What team characteristics do you and your team rate poorly?

If you were to pick one characteristic to work on collectively as a team, which would it be?

If you put these "team" wheels on a high performance car,

"How Smooth is Your Ride?"

Explore the Six Team Characteristics

Before we get into solution mode, let's learn more about each characteristic in detail and how it impacts you and your team.

As it was illustrated, each characteristic is equally important, thus the reason to use the spokes of a wheel analogy, but one of the characteristic, communication, is the glue that holds it all together. It's not more important, but its role is twofold, so it's put at the top of the list and is emphasized the most because its impact is greater and needs to be addressed first.

Communication:

Sign of the executive's desk:

"I know you believe you understood what you think I said, but I'm not sure you realize that what you heard is not what I meant to say."

The power of communication is limitless. To illustrate, I enjoy ethnic foods, especially Vietnamese cuisine. I make it a point to attempt to order my meal in their native language. When I first attempted this linguistic feat I got puzzled looks on my servers face, trying to figure out what am I talking about. Then when they see me pointing to the item on the menu while saying it in Vietnamese they immediately smile. They get that I'm attempting to order in their language and they're delighted. So much so, they sometimes invite the other restaurant workers over to hear my "American accent"

Get my personal help - See page 100 for details!

while speaking their language. What happens next is magic. All of a sudden, I'm accepted as one of them. I'm no longer the big white guy in the booth having lunch, I'm one of them. And the upside is every time I go back to this restaurant; they all remember me and give me the best seat in the house, the best service and the best food, all from taking the time to be in communication with them. So it doesn't have to be perfect to be effective.

There are many great training matrixes that explain how we communicate. In NLP, they talk about our communication tendencies, to give us awareness and predict how we might respond in certain situations. So we are broken down into one of the following, we are a visual person or we are an auditory person or we are a kinesthetic person and the acronym is VAK (Visual, Auditory or Kinesthetic). What makes knowing your communication tendencies so important is that it can cut down miscommunication drastically. For instance, my partner is aware that she is not just a visual person, but a high visual. What that means is that in a stressed situation, she will go to her strengths and in this case, that's high visual, blocking out all other communication styles except hers. She responds best to visual stimuli instead of words or feelings. So in an emergency, you would want to hold up a sign, wave your hands or write instructions to get her attention. You could give verbal instructions as much as you'd like until you're blue in the face, without any coherent response. So being aware of your communication tendencies is important.

Myers-Briggs® uses a communication style evaluation that describes our individual style with American Indian symbols. Like if you're an eagle, you tend to work as a visionary, or if you're a bear, you are the type that likes to accomplish projects.

And there are many more evaluations that tell us who we are and they can be very valuable for you to be aware of your tendencies. But for your teams and for the information in this book, I'm going to simplify it so we can put it into action quicker. The communication that we're concerned about is perspective.

My neighbor invited us over to watch the Lakers-Boston basketball finals and I asked if I could bring something over to feed everyone. Of course I got the nod to bring a main dish to the party, and they added that it's okay to try out something different on them.

Given the green light to try something new, I realized I had a hankering for lots of garlic. I then eyed a can of Burgundy snails (escargot for you Francophiles) in the pantry and a package of vermicelli pasta. Now the taste was rounding itself out quite nice but I needed to add some substance to the dish and remembered some great spicy Italian sausage that I just got at the meat market.

Well, if you'd ever had baked snails in garlic butter, this was what I was going after for flavor, add the pasta as filler and sliced, and spicy Italian sausage and you got a winner.

I got so involved with my pasta dish that I didn't realize the game had already begun. So we hurried over next door with my big bowl of pasta, neatly wrapped in plastic (great idea to keep it warm as well as in the bowl). Dropped off the pasta on the kitchen counter and joined my comrades on the sofa to cheer on our favorite team (I'll let you guess which one).

Soon, someone started to dish up the pasta and pass the plates around to all the gang. We were so wrapped up in the game; we didn't really talk much about the garlicky bowl of noodles that I brought over with me.

Fast forward to the conclusion of the night, everyone had a great time, they all appreciated the special dish that I brought over and then they started to ask, "What kind of mushrooms were in the pasta, they were delicious!"
I didn't understand right away what they meant until I got it, they thought the snails were "mushrooms"!

Well I explained what they really were and I apologized to the group for not communicating that important fact before we ate.

Of course I was forgiven by the gang, but I couldn't help thinking how similar this situation is in the work place. My miscommunication was based on perspective. From my perspective I thought it was totally normal to put snails in a pasta dish with lots of garlic. From my friend's perspective, mushrooms made more sense to go in this pasta dish. So they saw and tasted what they wanted to see and taste. Even though if you look and taste mushrooms and snails side by side, you could see the differences, taste the differences. But through our filters called perspective they were one in the same!

So it was a great reminder to me how important perspective is to effective communication. In our workshops, this is about the time I mention to the class, if you want to clean up your "perspective filters", ask clarifying questions. And keep asking until you have a sense of what the other persons perspective looks like (and tastes like!)

So the qualifying question I'll get next time I'm invited to bring over an unrecognizable ingredient is, "Is that snails in this dish?"

For a team, perspective plays an even bigger role in the success of the group. This can be the number one "blind spot" that holds your team back from being their full potential. By opening the door of awareness to the challenge of team perspective, your team will have a leg up on most other groups. As humans, we constantly create this illusion that everyone "gets us". But if we remind our teams that we need to constantly be in the present, be in the listening and be in the questions (clarifying), only then will we "get them" and what they really mean.

Collaboration:

A major reason capable people fail to advance is that they don't work well with their colleagues.
-Lee Iacocca

One of the biggest myths about creativity is that its source originates within those chosen few who access their artistic side of their mind best. Nothing can be further from the truth! True collaboration happens when the individual ego is set aside and the focus is placed on the team's outcome. Easier said than done!

As it was mentioned in the introduction, we are creatures of habit. We have been taught for years of pre-school, elementary school, junior high, high school, collage, both under graduate and post graduate that an idea is "our" idea. Our motivations, grades, bonuses, praise are all based on the individual ideas and achievement that we grind out throughout our lives and careers.

Then when we are asked to "collaborate" on a project that is bigger than us as individuals, no wonder we have conflict, confusion and poor results. It's not in our conditioning to work together on a common goal so why are we surprised?
Coming up with daily menus, specialties and promotions in a restaurant can be daunting and wear on the most creative person.   The worth of a great chef was on his or her creativity.   I was blessed very young with the passion, education and skill to come up with daily menus and

specialties during my first chef's job. I would arrive in the kitchens 3-4 hours earlier than any of the other cooks just so I had the extra time to plan these elaborate dishes. It wasn't until the birth of my son did I have to curtail the grueling schedule. I couldn't lower the standards of the specialties and menus coming out of the kitchen, but I couldn't devote the amount of time that I had devoted up until now.

It always seems in our desperation that we are forced to let go and change our habits and look to another way. I called upon my old friend and mentor, Gus. He always had the right thing to say for the right situations. He was my "Yoda" and his guidance always supported me well.

When I asked Gus what to do, how did he handle his family situations while owning and running his businesses, he responded with a question, "Where is your team?"
I asked, "What team?"

He asked again, "Where is your team, you played a variety of sports before knowing me, basketball, football, etc..., did you do them alone or did you have a team to support you?"

Once again, he reminded me of my power, my team, kitchen brigade. I thought I had to be the all-knowing chef so I could take all of the credit, just like how I was trained for years in school. It was time for a change and that's when our team creativity sessions began. I was no longer the only one who came up with all of the ideas, in fact, my role transformed more as a facilitator and coach than as the lone chef.

Get my personal help - See page 100 for details!

Collaboration became the norm and production soared. Because it was a collaboration, everyone felt a stronger sense of responsibility to the end result. I transformed my way of being forever.

Cooperation:

We should not only use the brains we have, but all that we can borrow.
-Thomas Woodrow Wilson

If you've ever had a great soup, most likely its base liquid component was a great stock. Whether it be a beef stock, poultry stock, shellfish stock or even vegetables stock, they all had one thing in common, a cooperation of flavors!

Cooperation's end result is that the outcome is greater the sum of its parts. This is especially true with soup stocks. A poultry stock, for example, is made up of the following: chicken bones, possible chicken meat trimmings, onion, celery, bay leaves, thyme and clear filtered water. Now each ingredient by itself is nothing special. But when you combine them together and apply slow steady heat, you transform these seven ingredients to a wonderful, savory soup broth that can be used for making soups, braised dishes, sauces or sautéed dishes. It's the power of combining these separate ingredients in cooperation to form something special.

As simple as the concept of cooperation may be, it is constantly overlooked because of our "these are my grades" conditioning for many years. The combined total results of a cooperative team are greater than the sum of its parts. Or another way of saying that is one plus one equals three which does not make sense to most individuals unless they have experienced it first-hand.

If you were fortunate to have been on a sports team that really stressed the team game, you'd know that it takes the entire team to win the game. Even great sports stars like Michael Jordan or Kobe Bryant know that they can't do it all. That they may have skills and gifts that put them in a whole other category of player than most, still they must have a full complement of team mates and role players to consistently win.

The cooperative team creates "synergy", working together, when present within a team construct, generates more of everything, more productivity, more enthusiasm, more connection.

Commitment:

The difference between "involvement" and "commitment" is like an eggs-and –ham breakfast: the chicken was "involved"—the pig was "committed". -Unknown

My first opportunity as a chef came when the owner of the restaurant I had been working, told me that he was making a change for the better and he wanted me to be a part of that change. When I found out that it involved my current chef was to be let go and I was offered the head chef's position, it scared me. I had never held that position before and I was concerned that I wasn't quite ready for this big step up.

After assurances from the owner that I was ready and that he would help me in my transition to head chef, I agreed.

The following week was a difficult one at best. I did not feel I was really in charge of the kitchen and I know I was no longer a part of the kitchen as a cook. It was the first time I truly experienced the term "limbo", one foot as the chef and the other as a one of the cooks and it showed in my work. Production was down, bad feelings among the crew were apparent because of me being the youngest in the kitchen, and there was no direction or connection with the service staff.

I soon was called into the owner's office and was asked what the problem was?

I said that I didn't know and that I was trying the best that I could to be the new chef.

He replied, "Maybe you should stop trying and start being the chef. It's time you jumped in with both feet and commit to who you really are right now!"

I took that advice to heart and committed to this leadership role and never looked back.

Get my personal help - See page 100 for details!

Commitment is the fuel that motivates and inspires a team. When a team is committed to itself, a project and each other, nothing cannot be achieved! When John F. Kennedy committed the United States to being the first people on the moon, it was as good as having happened. In fact, that is what happens with a team that is committed. By being committed to each other and to their team project, they put out such a strong intention that it is as good as being completed.

Commitment can't be faked. You either have it or you don't. To most teams, commitment preseeds trust, so many times you'll hear these terms as more of a phrase than individual words.

Trust:

The leaders who work most effectively, it seems to me, never say "I". And that's not because they have trained themselves not to say"I". They don't think "I", they think "we"; they think "team". They understand their job to be, to make the team function. They accept responsibility and don't sidestep it, but "we" gets the credit. This is what creates trust, what enables you to get the task done.
-Peter Drucker

This popular team characteristic brings me back to the most basic of team building exercises that sometimes becomes the butt of all team building jokes, the trust catch! If you're not familiar with the concept, it's where you stand on a platform a few feet off the ground with your back turned towards your team of 5-6 people. You then show your trust in the other members by falling backwards without looking behind you. They, intern do anything in their power to catch your falling body so it is cradled gently to ensure your safety.

The one fall back (pardon the pun :-)) to this exercise is that the metaphor is a quick, one time burst of profound trust that does not represent the real world. And I guess most of the participants that play this trust game understand that too because they usually joke about dropping you during the exercise with everyone knowing that would never happen. We all get that in an emergency, like when you are falling, that complete strangers will many times come to your rescue to prevent any harm to come to you.

But the trust we are talking about is based more on the day to day decision making. The trust we talk about is about profoundly knowing your team and putting the success of your team in their hands. By allowing them to believe, conceive and achieve the end result of their project. So it goes back to communication and staying in the conversation with each member to keep the trust alive.

One of the most difficult concepts that our host hotel chefs and our clients try to understand is how does a group complete through their team building program so successfully. When their goal is to create a multi-cultural gourmet buffet, how can we do this without recipes, without previous training and without proper kitchen facilities, yet

Get my personal help - See page 100 for details!

produce a fantastic outcome in a delicious gourmet buffet meal that would qualify for a four-star rating!

And this is done without the large amount of chef helpers that the host hotel chef would have provided and it is done without any pre-preparation of the food ingredients.

How can this be done?

Quite simply, trust! Trust from my culinary coaches that each team member, each individual team and the team as a whole wants this outcome as much as we do. Trust from the participants that we want them to be successful and are there to support them in their quest to their goal of a delicious buffet meal. Trust becomes a flow between the participants and the culinary coaches. Trust is the cornerstone in each team knowing that the other teams will produce a culinary product as high in standard as their own.

At first, it's difficult to master, trust. It's one of our "habits" to over control or another popular way to say it "micro-managing". But it's the key to experiencing one of our culinary team exercises and it's an invaluable lesson that is taken back to the workplace to implement.

Leadership:

The best executive is the one who has sense enough to pick good men to do what he wants done, and self-restraint to keep from meddling with them while they do it.
-Theodore Roosevelt

Get my personal help - See page 100 for details!

If communication is the glue that holds a team together, leadership is the characteristic that forges forward to the target in mind. A lot of myth surrounds the understanding of leadership like:

• Leaders are born not created
• There can only be one leader on a team
• Leaders lead from outside of the team, or
• Strong leadership is the only way to lead a team

While the truth of the matter is:

• Leadership is a learned skill that anyone can master
• Leadership is not just a position, it's a role played at any given time
• Leaders are a part of the team
• Leaders come in many shapes and sizes as does their leadership personalities, aggressive, analytical, passionate, understanding, etc...

So what is the one characteristic that all great leaders have in common, they are all in the listening! "Being in the listening" is beyond just listening. Being in the listening as a leader means that listening is a part of who you are as a leader, not just an act of doing. By understanding the equation of BE DO, then HAVE, where by being something comes first, that allows you to do something, in order to have something. If you change the equation to where it starts off as DO, HAVE, the BE or HAVE, DO, then BE, you'll never have consistency as a leader.

Get my personal help - See page 100 for details!

So to explain it simply, by BEING a wealthy person, you can DO the things wealthy people do thus HAVE the rewards that a wealthy person has (expensive cars, immense homes, etc...). But if you change the equation to first HAVING expensive luxury cars won't make you a wealthy person, just a person who has an expensive car! Or DOING the things that wealthy people do like travel to distant exotic retreats won't make you BE a wealthy person. BEING a wealthy person is not about your things or what you do. A wealthy person is a state of being that is as secure as a solid concrete and steel foundation. So Donald Trump is a wealthy person that when he was 900 million dollars in debt (that's well beyond broke!), he was still a wealthy person. This is what enabled him to quickly bounce back financially (HAVING) to where he is today as a billionaire. Or why the vast majority of lottery winners lose all of their money within a few years of attaining all of this money, they just didn't know how to BE wealthy, they just had money.

So BEING in the listening is the most important characteristic that a leader can be in order to be effective within a team. The captain of a ship may set the course, but it takes the whole crew to help stir the ship and stay the course.

One of our great military leaders of recent times is General Schwartzkopf. I had the privilege to hear him speak a few years after Desert Storm about leadership. A question from the audience asked him what was the most important trait that any leader must have to be effective? Immediately he replied, "Listening to the troops".

The general would explain that he would regularly walk among the troops to ask those questions or their opinions of situations that affect them right then. He knew that as a leader, his expertise was about setting the intention, the vision or the plan. He also was wise enough to know that his troops where the experts understanding "how" to carry out his plan. He got that he would sometimes have to get out of his own way and listen to his experts on how to best carry out his plan.

I was inspired by the simplistic way General Schwartzkopf connected the leadership/team concept. That any leader doesn't need to be the end all to knowing what to plan and how to carry out the plan, which was the beauty of his genius, it became our plan and not my plan.

So I needed to apply the new secret to my business immediately. Fortunately I had the perfect opportunity to test this new mindset. My business at the time was a high end French/Swiss restaurant and Valentine's Day was just around the corner. Typically Valentine's Day is a large volume day in many restaurants but even more so if you're a French style restaurant (ah, the romance of the French). So precise planning was the key to a very successful holiday for us. One of the challenges to a Valentine's Day was that most of the diners are couples that usually have somewhere to go after their dinner. So table turnover is key.

I decided to walk among my troops, the Mexican dishwashers on our staff and I asked them the question, "How would you organize and prepare for Valentine's Day business?"

Without hesitation, like they had been thinking a lot about this intense holiday situation, they immediately outlined a plan on how we can turn tables swiftly and effortlessly by hiring a temp worker, whose job was only to focus on the things that slow down the re-setting of the tables, not having enough clean and polished silverware and glasses. And to continue their plan, they suggested that we hire this person only from the most intense hours between 7pm and 10pm.

Well I followed my troop's plan of hiring one person with a singular focus and limited schedule. It worked! It worked like a charm so much so, that we stayed on schedule all night long so no couple had to wait for their table. So much so that we were able to accommodate other couples who had no reservations thus maximizing revenues. So much so that the dining staff was able to reset the dining room for the next day and leave hours earlier than normal because of no delays thus saving on labor costs. And if I hadn't listened to them, I would have done what I always had done, hire a temporary dishwasher for the whole night without any special focus thus wasting more money and time! Listening to my troops really paid off!

Get my personal help - See page 100 for details!

Chapter Three:

When Your Team Doesn't Perform Like a Team

Chapter Three:

When Your Team Doesn't Perform Like a Team

Effective teamwork will not take the place of knowing how to do the job or how to manage the work. Poor teamwork, however, can prevent effective final performance. And it can also prevent team members from gaining satisfaction in being a member of a team and the organization.
-Robert F. Bales

The Five Pitfalls of NOT having an effective team:

Everyone will agree that having a team is important to any company, organization or even family. Unfortunately most of these same people that agree that having a team is important are the same people that don't support their team's formations thus never really benefiting from the full potentials of a team.

Now I don't blame them because once again, it's not our fault. We are human and as humans we are creatures of habit. Our habits have been formed and anchored in us for many years since our youth up until now. And like creating great leaders, building and supporting teams is a learned skill that was absent from our formative years and fortified in our adulthood. So it's not our fault up until now, because we now know better.

Five Dysfunctions of a team:

1. Lack of production
2. Increased turnover
3. Lack of connectivity in the job
4. Lack of commitment to your cause
5. The "Being" of a company that produces poor service and/or poor products

Lack of Production:

Imagine the Vikings rowing their sleek battle ships with only one side of the ship properly using their oars correctly. Where would they go?

Well they'd most likely go in circles or they'd travel completely off course from their original plan at best!
Maybe your teams occasionally go in circles or off course too?

Lack of production not only hurts the bottom line of your organization, it fortifies the "being" of your team to guarantee "off course" production results in the future. Remember, we're creatures of habit and without intervention, habits continue until it becomes the culture of your organization. This is where you hear phrases like, "It's the way we've always done it" or "If it worked that way before, just keep doing it again" or the most famous, "If it ain't broke, why fix it?"

Off production can be so sneaky if we get what we have always expected. If we expect the average production of a team, that is exactly what we'll get. Remember, the habit has been created and without being shaken up, it'll continue.

During one of our family gatherings when I was young, my Mom was preparing the family pot roast for that night's family celebration meal. I watched as she carefully put the pot roast together as she had done at least a hundred times before. This being my first time actually watching the process from the beginning, I noticed that the two ends of the pot roast where trimmed off.

I curiously asked, "Mom, why did you trim off the ends of the pot roast?"

My Mom said that it was how she learned it from her Mom and suggested that I ask my Grandma who was in the next room.

So I approached my Grandma and asked, "Grandma, I noticed that my Mom trimmed the ends off of the pot roast before putting in the oven, she said she learned that from you and that you'd tell me why it done that way?"

Well Grandma replied very much like my Mom replied that she had learned how to cook pot roast from her Mom and to learn why, just go ask Great Grandma in the next room."

Get my personal help - See page 100 for details!

I approached my Great-Grandma just as I had done with my Grandma and Mom about why we trim off the ends of the pot roast?

Well, Great-Grandma just thought for a moment, probably recalling the specific cooking technique that I was asking about when she replied, "Well, the reason why we would trim the pot roast was quite simple, back then, the braising pan that I used to cook the pot roast was too small, so I trimmed off the ends so it would fit the pan."

Increased Turnover:

According to William G. Bliss of Bliss and Associates, Inc.
The following is a comprehensive checklist of items to include when calculating the cost of turnover in any organization. To determine the costs, have the hourly and weekly cost of fully loaded payroll costs (i.e. salary plus benefits) of the vacant position, the management staff, the recruitment staff and others as outlined below.

It should be noted that the costs of time and lost productivity are no less important or real than the costs associated with paying cash to vendors for services such as advertising or temporary staff. These are all very real costs to the employer.

These calculations will easily reach 150% of the employees' annual compensation figure. The cost will be significantly higher (200% to 250% of annual compensation) for managerial and sales positions.

To put this into perspective, let's assume the average salary of employees in a given company is $50,000 per year. Taking the cost of turnover at 150% of salary, the cost of turnover is then $75,000 per employee who leaves the company. For the mid-sized company of 1,000 employees who has a 10% annual rate of turnover, the annual cost of turnover is $7.5 million!

Do you know any CEO who would want to add $7.5 million to their revenue? And, by the way, most of that figure would be carried over to the profits line as well. What about the company with 10,000 employees? The cost of turnover equals $75 million!

Calculating and adding all these costs, given our original example of the $50,000 person can easily reach $75,000 to replace them. As you can see, the costs and impact associated with an employee who leaves the company can be quite significant. This is not to say that all turnovers should be eliminated. However, given the high cost and impact on running a business, a well thought-out program designed to retain employees may easily pay for itself in a very short period of time.

At one time in a company, you would hear this phrase coming from the sales department, "It's a numbers game!", referring to the high number of prospects you need to go through before you closed a sale. Well that same phrase is being used more often in different department, human resources!

There is always a certain amount of attrition within any company or organization. But it seems that the norm is to over-hire, knowing that many will leave thus referring to it as "the numbers game".

It's much easier to abandon a job if there is nothing to lose and that it won't impact anyone except yourself briefly. It's much easier to walk away from a faceless entity rather than the face of your teammates who depend on your input.

The cost of bringing on a new employee is skyrocketing and that is an investment that will never pay-off.

Lack of Connectivity in the Workplace:

One of the biggest buzz words in companies is the term "employee engagement" which simply means an engaged employee is a person who is fully involved in and enthusiastic about their work.

And according to Blessing White's 2008 Employee Engagement Executive Report -

Engaged employees are not just committed. They are not just passionate or proud. They have a line-of-sight on their own future and on the organization's mission and goals. They are

Get my personal help - See page 100 for details!

"enthused" and "in gear" using their talents and discretionary effort to make a difference in their employer's quest for sustainable business success.

This feeling of being connected to the business relies on the relationship's that are forged at the workplace. The more friends and relationships that are created at the workplace, the more commitment employees show to do well, stay longer and produce more on the job.

According to a report by the Hay Group found that offices with engaged employees were up to 43% more productive!

So there is a direct correlation between the people in your team being connected to each other, creating close friendships, being connected to the mission and goals of your organization to increased productivity.

Lack of Commitment:

Whoever said anybody has a right to give up?
-Marian Wright Edelman

One of the most brutal sports that I did not take up in my youth, by the urging of my mother (thanks Mom!) was the sport of boxing. Even though I don't partake in the sport, I do appreciate what it takes to compete in these matches.

One of the characteristics that is common among all boxing champions is the total commitment to their ability to beat their opponent. You've seen it even after a fight is completed and the boxer who just lost will still insist that they were not defeated.

George Foreman during his first reign as world champion was beat by Mohammed Ali, who first coined the term, "rope a dope" as a tactic to beat the champ. Years later during an interview, it was learned that what beat George Foreman was not his body giving out from intense stress of the hot, humid weather and the overexertion in punching the challenger. But it was that sliver of doubt that crippled his chances to stay champion. His lack of commitment in his ability to beat the former champion is what really defeated him that evening.

You get what you focus on and in business, if your team focuses on doubt, poor results will follow. RAS or reticular activating system is exactly that, what you continually focus on is what you'll continually see. As a team, that fact is magnified exponentially. If there is a lack of commitment, to the team, towards the project or towards your company, all will be sabotaged. When a team is in this state, it is very difficult to get them out of it. It becomes a spiral downward away from your initial objectives toward the profound doubt that the team now focuses.

This is why inconsistency in the messages given will feed that doubt and cripple the direction that their project is going and ultimately, the course of the company. So lack of commitment quickly becomes insufficient productivity and poor morale.

The "Being" of a Company that Produces Poor Services/ Products:

Our achievements of today are but the sum total of our thoughts of yesterday. You are today where the thoughts of yesterday have brought you and your will be tomorrow where the thoughts of today take you.
-Blaise Pascal

Nothing is more critical to any entity, individual or organization than your respective core identification or otherwise known as your state of "being". All decisions, ideas, action plans and more importantly, behavior are dictated by your core identification.

Most companies work diligently to clarify their organizations core identification through their mission statement, company purpose, brand and top values. But with all of that work, many times these words are lost as it is filtered throughout the company and these important documents never become the essence or "being" of your organization. Or part of your organization, usually the part more closely connected to your mission "get it" while pockets of departments run things their own way.

Either way, the results are noticeable when you connect with your customers, patients or clients and they don't receive what your sales team promised or your expensive marketing campaigns promise. Then it becomes a customer service issue instead of a "state of being" issue. What follows is an

Get my personal help - See page 100 for details!

expensive array of putting out fires and quick fixes that never address the core problem, a confused state of being!

Once this confusion happens in any organization, it spreads like a malignant cancer. And like a cancer, it's usually treated by "cutting out" the infected parts instead of transforming the environment to support your core identification.

As you can see, running any company, organization or family can cost you much in profits, productivity and relationships.

Any business is susceptible to a confused or non-existent core state of being. After the sale of one of Silicon Valley's premier restaurants, this very issue took hold with the new owners. Even though after the completion of the sale, everything was in place exactly as it was before the sale, same staff, same menu, same hours, same advertising, even the same recipes; what was different was a profound change of the core state of being of the restaurant. First slowly, then more regularly, key employees would leave, volume of customers would diminish, quality control slipped far below standards and overall revenues dropped!

Of course, the new owners didn't stand by while this was happening. They did what most people would do, address and put out the most recent fires burning (not literally!) They spend their days in a total reactionary state of being. Never addressing the center of all of their woes, lack of a core state of being, something you can't just purchase in a business transaction.

The last that was heard about this business was that they were purchasing barely enough food to complete one

Get my personal help - See page 100 for details!

evening dinner service and had to turn away a table of eight late night diners because of lack of food!

What Do You Want to Change?

Out of these five dysfunctions, which one spoke to you the loudest?

If you asked your team, which of the five dysfunctions would they choose?

Is the team dysfunction that you picked the same as the other members of you team might have picked?

List in order which dysfunctions you'd like to eliminate first:
1. _____
2. _____
3. _____
4. _____
5. _____

Chapter Four:

Transform Your Team Through TAC™

Chapter Four:

Transform Your Team through TAC™

"Carefully watch your THOUGHTS, for they become your WORDS. Manage and watch you WORDS, for they will become your ACTIONS. Consider and judge your ACTIONS, for they have become you HABITS. Acknowledge and watch your HABITS, for they shall become your VALUES. Understand and embrace you VALUES, for they become YOUR DESTINY."
-Mahatma Gandhi

How do you get your teams to operate at high efficiency? How do you eliminate your team's "blind spots" and allow them to operate at their full potentials?

In his book, Getting Engaged: The New Workplace Loyalty, author Tim Rutledge explains that truly engaged employees are attracted to, and inspired by, their work ("I want to do this"), committed ("I am dedicated to the success of what I am doing"), and fascinated ("I love what I am doing")
The problem that most of us face is that we are human; therefore we are creatures of habit. And unless we are forced to change, we will continue to do what we do, no matter if it supports us or not.

The creation of habits is not exclusive to the human race. In the animal kingdom, we use the creation of habits to train animals to "be" a certain way around us. For instance, the way an elephant is conditioned to not roam around in the circus grounds, starts at an early age. When the elephant is young, a chain is attached to the baby elephant's leg and the other end is firmly secured with a stake planted deep in the ground. Because the baby elephant is too immature to break free of the metal chain, it soon stops struggling and accepts that it is unable to release itself. As the elephant grows and matures, its metal chain is replaced with a light rope that could be easily snapped by the animal at any time. But because of the elephant's long time conditioning and deep seeded habit of being secured, it will not break free and will continue being attached as long as it feels the rope on its leg.

The most effective way to transform any group is to interrupt the unwanted conditioning and replace it with a more supporting pattern of being. One way of doing this is through TAC™ or Team Associative Conditioning, which is a fancy way of saying that we take any team, scramble their paradigm or belief of who they are and imprint over them a new blueprint of being that builds relationships, empowers creativity and innovation and overall changes the course of your organization forever!

TAC™ Steps Involved:

The process of transforming a team is the following:

- Identify what six team characteristics not performing to a higher standard
- Identify what five pitfalls your team has succumbed
- Scramble you team's paradigm
- Replace it with a new, empowering paradigm of being

Get my personal help - See page 100 for details!

- Anchor-in this new state of being
- Follow up

The success of this process is determined by the steps taken in the proper order and completing the steps in their entirety.

Identify the "bumps" in the Road:

In chapter two, we described an analogy of taking the six characteristics that make up a high performance team and giving each characteristic a value that corresponds to the length of a spoke of a wagon wheel. We asked the question, how smooth would your ride be? Would it be smooth, slightly bumpy or does it feel like there are massive gaps in the wheel that would throw you off a wagon if you used these wheels underneath you?

Even good teams that have worked together may have some bumps in their ride. Taking an inventory of how your team characteristic rate is just like any good reporting system, it give you an indication on where you are or may be headed. Use this as a tool to help in evaluating the potentials of your team without any bias. Where the biggest bumps are is an indication on where to begin.

Use the following illustration to fill in the length of the spokes by shading in your rating. Use the rating of 1 to 10,

1 being poor to 10 being excellent. Remember, this is just a tool to help you identify where to begin our focus.

This tool can be used from a singular view point or a 360° view point and given to everyone on the team. Here are some questions below to help you with your evaluations:

Rate each section from 1 (answers being poor) to 10 (answers being excellent)

Communication _____.
Are you and your team being in the listening most of the time?
Is the communication within your group flow consistently?
Do you feel that your communication is a "blind spot" keeping you from maximizing your team's productivity?

Collaboration _____.

Do you observe that your creativity is being best used by the team through collaborative efforts?
When a team member is in a stuck place, do they use others in the team to get un-stuck?
Is your team proactive in collaborating on ideas to complete your project quicker or more creatively?

Cooperation _____.

Do your team members generate an environment of cooperation?

Get my personal help - See page 100 for details!

Do you create results as a team greater than the sum of what you can achieve individually?

Does everyone on your team embrace cooperation to maximize your results?

Commitment _____.

From your observation, are your team members committed to their team, project and company?

Is your team fully supported in their project by their company?

Is your team excited about their project?

Trust _____.

Do you trust that all members of your team will complete their part of their project?

Do your team members communicate well with each other?

Do your team members know each other outside of work or projects?

Leadership _____.

Does your team have a clear vision of their project or outcomes?

Is their more than one person capable to lead the team?

Is everyone on the team "heard" by the leadership?

Now take a look at the wagon wheel spokes that you have made and sketch a line to connect the outside of your wheel spokes to form the tire wheel around the spokes. Ask yourself the question, "From the wheels that I just made, how smooth is my ride?" If the wheel that is formed is a smooth ride, but it's not a very large wheel, ask yourself, "How fast can I travel with small sized wheels?" And if you have large gaps of missing spokes, you need to restore the integrity of your wheel and team immediately before more damage is done!

You may have two spokes that are smaller than you would like, which one do you address first? From experience, we have found that all of these characteristics are connected, so healing one will many times influence another. If one of the two spoke characteristics is communication, I would focus my attention on that. As mentioned during the descriptions of these team characteristics, communication is the glue that holds all of these characteristics together. So by focusing on communication first will help in improving all of the areas, especially the other characteristic that is noticeably insufficient.

If there are two characteristics spokes that include the leadership characteristic, look to see if there is a lack of vision or purpose for the team. Lack of a clear vision will affect all of the other characteristics and will show itself as a "symptom" rather than the cause. An example would be if two spoke characteristics were leadership and commitment, the symptom would be commitment, but the root cause is a lack of clarity in the vision or purpose which would fall under lack of leadership.

Get my personal help - See page 100 for details!

The spokes of the wheel exercise/illustration is just a visual aid to assist in determining the fastest and most efficient approach to determining what action to take next. If you need more help in determining what area or approach to begin with in transforming your team, the next section may help you determine your direction from the angle of what has already happened and are considered the pitfalls.

Identify the Pitfalls:

When you use the previous spoke team characteristic model to determine what area you want to focus on first approach, some of the results of a deficiency of these characteristic has not shown up yet. So it you have determined what team characteristic(s) is deficient for your team, there is no need to continue to identify your pitfalls. But when these results do show up in the form of these team pitfalls, it now becomes very obvious that your team is in trouble. This evaluation is to be used to only identify what obvious pitfalls have seeped into your team. This is not to be done to identify the group as it is their core identity or look at one of these pitfalls as the problem. Look at these pitfalls without any judgment or meaning to them and treat them more like a symptom that they experiencing and not the cause. By identifying the symptom for some, will help them reverse engineer to which characteristic(s) are being challenged in your team.

Below are some questions that will help you determine if any or all of the pitfalls apply to your team:

Lack of Production:

Has there been a sudden drop in the teams output?
Has there been a consistent decrease of production from each quarter?
Have there been consistent delays due to poor planning?

Increased Turnover:

Has there been a sudden loss of team members?
Have there been consistent delays due to lack of available team members?
Has there been consistent drop in production due to a shortage of good workers?

Lack of Connectivity:

Is there unusual amount of friction among your team?
Do you notice team members avoiding each other regularly?
Is there one or two people ignored or left out, shunned by the rest of the team?

Lack of Commitment:

Do you find members of your team generally disinterested in your project or company?
Is there consistent tardiness, absences or key team members MIA during critical milestones of a project?
Does work look incomplete, sloppy or non-existent?

The "State of Being" of your Company that Produces Poor Service and/or Poor Products:

Do you often hear the phrase, "That's just how it is around here"?

Is it <u>not</u> shocking to receive complaints about your services and/or products?

Do rumors abound around and about your company that are not true, half true or are questionably true?

Circle or write down the questions that seem to apply most to your situation. Look for a common pattern in these pitfalls that keep pointing towards a lack of a particular team characteristic. For instance, a lack of enthusiasm for a project has produced short comings in revenue or productivity which created a core identity or state of being for this team as not caring. One team characteristic that may be lacking, in this instance, is leadership, by not creating a clear vision for the team to follow. This unclear vision or path promotes a lack of enthusiasm within the team, which causes a lack of production or revenues and ultimately the team is branded as a group of uncaring slack-offs.

Every team pitfall can be traced back to one or two team characteristics that need to develop. But before it can be developed, a new state of being needs to be inserted and before that, the group needs to collectively be redesigned and scrambled to prepare to be transformed.

Get my personal help - See page 100 for details!

Scramble Your Teams Paradigm:

No, this is not "brain washing", it's more like "brain confusion". We want your team to remember their old behavior, well at first maybe, just so they can compare the differences between the old team and the transformed team. These are a critical step in the transformation process and if you needed a metaphor to illustrate what we do, think back to the time when we played music on records. You remember back in the day, those large plastic discs that play recorded music by placing a stereo needle into the grooves of the record and amplifying the sounds. If you wanted to distort the sounds that were produced by the record, so you couldn't recognize the original recorded music, one way to distort would be to get a nail and scratch the surface of the record. One time scratching would make the music skip, but if you continue to scratch over and over, the original sounds would be unplayable and unrecognizable.

The scratching of the record album is an interruption of a pattern. If you can dissipate patterns, you can deal with anything! And if you break a pattern often, creatively, or intense enough, it will eventually break. To interrupt your team's pattern you must simply break a team's habitual focus!

A simple way to illustrate an example of scrambling a pattern is to pour yourself a glass of milk and as you are drinking your milk, think of it instead as a glass of juicy, fresh squeezed lemon juice? You may experience a smooth, cool, slightly sweet taste in your mouth at first, but when you imagine an acidic tasting glass of lemon juice, arg!, it bothers me right now and I'm not even drinking milk! It interrupts your "milk taste" pattern to the point where you stop drinking the milk until you get that "taste" out of your mouth! This pattern interrupt works best when the lemon juice suggestion is done as a surprise by someone else. But if you are fully associated with the impact of drinking a whole glass of fresh lemon juice you'll start producing saliva immediately, with or without drinking anything!

Another popular pattern interrupt is to wear a rubber band around your wrist to help you to stop thinking or focusing on an unwanted habit, experience or person. Anytime you catch yourself thinking of that respective situation, you snap the rubber band, interrupting the thought. This is continued until the unwanted habit is associated with the unpleasant feeling of the rubber band stinging your skin and you drop that habit.

What works for individual pattern interrupts can work for teams as well. And to be most effective in scrabbling the group's pattern, the following steps should be weaved together:

- It must be outrageous
- It must be inclusive
- It must be elegant

Get my personal help - See page 100 for details!

It Must Be Outrageous

A team must be surprised or overwhelmed to get their attention and have the scramble work best. You can use outrageous questions like, "What time will you burp tomorrow afternoon?", or visualization pattern interrupt techniques or transformational vocabulary interrupts. The most effective scrambling techniques for teams that I have found are stories and actual kinesthetic experiences. Doing something that gets the team fully associated physically into the activity and that challenges your team is best. It's an activity that is totally engaging, enjoyable and has an outcome, conclusion or point to be experienced. This type of team experience becomes a collective, shared scrambling or pattern interrupt.

It Must Be Inclusive

The team experience must be one that everyone can do. The challenge with experiencing a pattern interrupt with a group, is knowing that the most effective interruptions should match the communication mode that we associate best. So individually, if we are a more visual person, visual pattern interrupts would work more effectively for us. But within a group, you will have a mix of different sensing pattern modes, so you need to have an experience that covers visual people, auditory people and kinesthetic people. This would truly be an effective shared experience pattern interrupt that would immediately bring the team together in great rapport with each other.

Get my personal help - See page 100 for details!

It Must Be Elegant

Once again, to be most effective with a diverse group, your experience must be something that fits the group. It can be outrageous and inclusive while being elegant. If your experience is outrageous for the sake of outrageousness, it might not be elegant, which would not be inclusive. If your experience is physical, but to the point where most of the group felt left out because it was too physical, that wouldn't be elegant nor bring your group to rapport. Would it be an effective pattern interrupt, absolutely! But it would be only a short term pattern interrupt and we are looking for long term change through rapport building.

Once the pattern interrupt has done its job, in many cases transformation has already happened. The experience is so powerful, because it is experienced by the whole team; it intensifies exponentially to facilitate team transformation! Many times teams will know what to do with this renewed place of transformation. But to be totally effective this is when you can replace those group beliefs.

Replace it with a new, empowering paradigm of being:

The future is not a result of choices among alternative paths offered by the present, but a place that is created —created first in the mind and will, created next in activity. The future is not some place we going to, but one we are creating. The paths are not to be found, but made, and the activity of making them, changes both the maker and the destination.
-John Schaar

Get my personal help - See page 100 for details!

This is the next step in fully transforming your team. Once we have eliminated your team's old pattern, now is the time to provide an alternative state of being. This is where your team comes from a place of "nothingness" or clean slate and is the perfect place to create a new team possibility of being. This is also the time that the benefits of this new state of being are brought out. The best way to do this is by asking questions that match the state of being of your team. The questions are related to the success your team experienced during their scrabble experience. Here are some examples of possible questions:

Communication:

How did the group communicate with each other?
Was the group effective in its communication with one another?
Which communication methods worked best? Which were least effective?
Give examples of successful communication.
What makes effective communication?

Leadership:

Was there a group leader? How was she/he selected?
What was the leadership method the leader used?
Did you feel the leader heard everyone?
Was there a clear vision or purpose for the team?

Cooperation:

How effective was the cooperation between team members?
Were there any team members who were more cooperative/
less cooperative than others?

Trust:

How well did team members trust each other?
How was trust demonstrated within the team?

Commitment:

What did you team experience from being committed and
attaining success as a team?
What did you gain from experiencing high commitment
from your team?

Collaborate:

How did your team members collaborate on improving on
your team outcome?
Did collaboration with team members improve your
innovation efforts to a better outcome?

Anchor in this new state of being:

*Each of us literally chooses, by his way of attending to
things, what sort of universe he shall appear to himself
to inhabit.*
-William James

Get my personal help - See page 100 for details!

Now that a new state of being, a blueprint to your teams paradigm of being, now is the time to anchor this into the team. Three techniques of anchoring work best with a team:

- Rehearsal
- Preframe and/or reframe
- Reinforcement

Rehearsal:

Rehearsal begins when members of the team respond to the lessons learned and the questions asked. If the pattern scrambler was the experience of learning to "be" as a team, then the rehearsal is the reminder of what the team experienced collectively. This rehearsal benefits them through repetition and for when they are together in the real world and surrounded by all of the challenges that could remind them of who they were as a team before transformation. The repeated rehearsal anchors in how they chose to be, as a team despite those challenges. Rehearsal is a way the team can condition themselves as a transformed team. With repetition, the brain begins to believe that the constructed state of being is a memory stored as a past reference thus anchoring this new paradigm of being.

Preframe and/or Reframe:

This anchoring technique can be used in its entirety or singularly. Focus equals reality, meaning determines emotions and perception determines behavior.

Preframing is used to prepare the team to the conditions that they may encounter in the real world of challenges. It helps them prepare in a safe environment of who they will be in challenging circumstances.

Reframe is giving the group a new frame of reference to who they are collectively and what they can accomplish collectively.

Reinforcement:

This is to create consistency in behavior. Any behavior that is accurately reinforced will grow and expand. This is used to remind the team of what they can accomplish and their unlimited potentials in this new state of being. This is also the time to remind them of what they get as benefits in this new state of being so the team is gaining something pleasurable. This will take the place of what the team perceived as benefits before transformation so there is no collective experience of loss. And as humans, we are always motivated by going towards pleasure and avoiding pain.

Follow Up:

Up until now, transformation has been accomplished at one place in time and the real world awaits our team; even though transformation of a team is a powerful experience that usually stays with a team for a long time. Good follow up tools ensure that the team stays transformed no matter what outside influences persist. Below is a list of tools that can be employed to keep your team in this new state of being.

Get my personal help - See page 100 for details!

- Transformational Vocabulary
- Coaching
- Auditory Triggers
- Physical Triggers
- Visual Triggers
- Shared Experiences

Transformational Vocabulary:

Transformational vocabulary refers to habitual words that we use to describe our experiences. As a team, this can become our "in house" terminology or slang. Words and phrases should be evaluated by the team to determine the impact those "in house" words on the team's new state of being. These words are powerful biochemical triggers that distort, delete or generalize our collective experiences. A new, more effective set of words and phrases can be utilized to take the place of the old words and phrases that no longer support the team's new state of being. An example of transforming words to be more empowering would be, instead of, "I have a problem" to I have a challenge" or "you really piss me off!" to "I'm really peeved by your behavior!" By changing the words that you have habitually used to a new set of thought out words, you won't react in same way you had during pre-transformation. In most cases, those reactions where over the top and never reflected what was really happening; so eliminating the old habitual words, deflates the intense energy surrounding them and by replacing them with new, more beneficial words that open up new possibilities.

Get my personal help - See page 100 for details!

Coaching:

Coaching is a great way to not only remind the team of their profound transformation, but also track the many successes that the team has created along the way. Any great athlete will tell you that by themselves, they can only reach a certain level of success, but with the right coaching, they reach levels thought not possible. The power is that the coach is instructing, inspiring, encouraging and caring from the place of your teams new state of being. So the coach is coming from a place of unlimited potentiality. So anything else would be alien.

Auditory Triggers:

We don't realize that some of the most powerful triggers we have are connected to what we hear. As a test, pull out a dance song that you really enjoyed from your early high school years and play it. Beyond you getting up to boogie to the music, be present to the other feelings, pictures and memories that stream into your head. Advertisers have known this for years. In fact, next time you watch a commercial ad on television, notice the type and time era of the music paired up the project. It'll tell you immediately who the prime demographics that make up the customers for this product. An example has been Cadillac cars being promoted to the baby boom generation with Rock & Roll music by Led Zeppelin playing as the car zips around tight corners. Before that commercial, most Baby Boomers considered Cadillac something their parents would drive, now Led Zeppelin music has made it okay to drive. If a music playlist was used during your team's transformation, use it as often as possible to bring your team back to the moment and remind them of who they are as a transformed team. Play the music at meetings, get-togethers, even at the office Monday morning before it gets hectic on the phones.

Physical Triggers:

Have you ever had a souvenir from a ball game or a concert and every time you would wear the t-shirt or hat, you couldn't help remembering the event. That's what a physical trigger can do for your team. Help them remember the transformational experience through having some item or items to trigger the time. Hats, t-shirts, aprons, coffee mugs, anything that is used regularly and symbolizes the moment can bring you back to the moment.

If it's a piece of clothing, it would be great to have the whole team wear during important production or planning meetings to remind the group of who they are transformed.

Also, by hanging around the very people you transformed with is a powerful trigger because of the shared experience. You are the culmination of the five people that you spend your most time with! Think about that and take inventory of whom and how much time you spend with people that support who you have transformed to. If your team is a department at work and the other departments have not experienced transformation yet, be wary of the time you spend with them unless they support your changes. If your family team has created a new empowering state of being, search out others who have done the same to support your efforts. It's worth losing a few old friends if they are not willing to transform themselves and their team because they will just want to drag you down.

Visual Triggers:

Pictures and photographs are very powerful visual triggers and during the transformational process should be taken abundantly. Especially if a common outcome has been achieved to show the power that the transformed team owns. Pictures can be posted in a common area in an office situation or they can be emailed with important messages or a slide show can precede gatherings and meetings to trigger the best of the transformed team.

Sometime symbols are created during your team's transformation; this symbol can be very powerful, like a team brand and should be hung in common areas and included in communications.

Shared Experiences:

Shared experiences are the best way to trigger your team's experience in transformation. The actual experience that helped you transform is the one that must be repeated. Teams grow, people move on naturally and you want to always improve upon what you have achieved as a team. So use the tool that worked in the first place to assist in your team's transformation.

Your team must experience this common challenge at a minimum of once a year with smaller shared experiences throughout the year to connect everyone. Many teams are geographically challenged and physically being with each other may not be possible but once a year. If that's the case, use opportunities to have a conference call or webinar to bring the team together. The more created you become, the more appreciative the team becomes of your efforts.

First say to yourself what you would be: and then do what you have to do.
-Epictetus

Chapter Five:

What Are Your Choices?

Chapter Five:

What are your Choices?

When you make an efficient choice in moments of indecision, you establish more effectiveness within a given time span, saving energy and stress. That's a time shift.
-Doc Childre, Freeze-Frame

The steps are clear on why and how to create a new paradigm of being for your team. Now is the choice of what would be the best method for your team to experience. Some key factors must be considered before you decide.

First, they must match the basic TAC® Team Associative Conditioning plan to achieve transformation for your team. If you encounter any program that promises change for your team, make sure that at least the steps that we outlined for you are included that plan. Here is a checklist to make sure that they are included:

- ✓ Identify what six team characteristics are not performing to a higher standard
- ✓ Identify what five pitfalls your team has succumbed
- ✓ Scramble your team's paradigm
- ✓ Replace it with a new, empowering paradigm of being
- ✓ Anchor in this new state of being
- ✓ Follow up

Get my personal help - See page 100 for details!

If any of these steps are missing, then keep moving on to a program that can promise you these steps or ones very similar are being used.

Another important point that must be addressed that was alluded to in the "scramble your team's paradigm" section was there must be rapport with the program type and your team. Programs must match up with the type of team that you have, their personalities, their intelligence, their emotional intelligence, their physicality, their cognitive skills and interpersonal skills.

For instance, a very popular team transformational program during the 80's and 90's was ropes courses. A good ropes course would challenge a team to greater height's (pardon the pun!) by having them perform tasks 50 feet above the ground. A professionally run ropes course can use all of the TAC™ characteristics but one, building rapport. Currently we have an overabundance of Baby Boomers in management in our workforces whose athletic prowess is quite a few years behind them and so are many of their workers. A rope course for this group would be disastrous. They would focus so much on their own physical limitations or challenges that even if they did complete the program, they would miss the whole point of doing this as a team. So no team transformation would happen, maybe personal transformation, but not team.

This goes for river rafting or even sailing, all great metaphors that I have even referenced in this book, but if all of your team is not physical, you are immediately putting a wedge between the physical people and the non-physical. Rapport between your team and the program does not happen and ultimately neither does transformation. So be very aware of who the members of your team before making that most critical choice.

What does transcend all cultural barriers is music and food! They challenge a team in a much different way than the more physical type team programs and if they follow the TAC™ list of steps (see above), you will achieve team transformation and create a new, empowering team state of being that will benefit you, your team, your business and/or your organization.

Below is a list of popular team development programs with their respective pros and cons. For suggestions to reputable companies in the area of your interest, please call our offices for an up-to-date referral – call toll free 888-308-TEAM (8326):

Ropes Courses	**Battle Simulations**
Scavenger Hunts	**Team Orientations**
River Rafting	**Team Sailing**
Culinary Challenges	**Music & Rhythm**
Mystery Theatre	**Motivational Speaking**
Indoor Team Games	**Outdoor Team Games**

Get my personal help - See page 100 for details!

Ropes Courses:

Pros-In the right hands can be a very powerful pattern interrupt and can apply the TAC™ steps to team transformation. Though I find ropes courses more of an excellent personal development tool, in the right hands, and the right team collective focus, success can be had.

Cons- Inclement weather and seasonability could limit your team's ability to plan accordingly.

Battle Simulations:

Pros- Able to fit within all of the TAC® steps of transformation with the right company. Fairly intense pattern interrupt. Works well in a hotel or conference meeting situation so environment can be controlled (no weather delays)

Cons- Questionable climate with some companies and organizations and the people within those organizations who are not too keen on the battle/war scenario. The potential violence theme could turn off many in your team thus inhibiting your team's transformation.

Scavenger Hunts:

Pros- Fun way to get your team to function as a unit. Best suggestion would be for a less important follow up team get-together after the initial team transformation. Can be done indoors (museums) or outdoors (famous or historical city)

Con-The fact that your whole team is usually split up and don't see each other during the whole process makes this a poor team transformational program. Also most scavenger hunts are not designed with team transformation in mind.

Team Orientation:

Pros- Much more techy with more companies using GPS toys to aid their participants through the thickest of woods or confusing city center. Questionable whether true transformation can be achieved but a good follow up program after team transformation has been achieved.

Con-Like scavenger hunts, the team is physically out of touch with the smaller teams until they find home base.

River Rafting:

Pros-In the right hands can be a very powerful pattern interrupt and can apply the TAC™ steps to team transformation. Depending on the river and time of the year, many teams would benefit to going outdoors to a very natural environment.
Cons- Depending on the river and time of year, it could negatively affect part of your team's ability to bond in rapport towards transformation.

Get my personal help - See page 100 for details!

Team Sailing:

Pros- In the right hands can be a very powerful pattern interrupt and can apply the TAC™ steps to team transformation. A very good metaphor if used in the right hands.

Cons- Be very wary of who is running the sailing. You don't want just any old skipper; you want a training company that knows sailing and all of its intricacies. Limited number to how many can participate at one time. Also, sea sickness can ruin the whole team experience. Best used as a team experience, not the team experience.

Culinary Challenges:

Pros- One of the experiences that transcend cultural barriers so in this work world of diversity; cultural, age, gender, it works extremely well. In the right hands can be one of the most powerful transformational experiences because of the inclusion of all the senses, visual, auditory, kinesthetic as well as a few that no other program type has, olfactory and gustatorial, which is extremely important with regards to both transformation and anchoring the transformation. It also puts all of the participants on an even playing field so no person as an unfair advantage over another. So if your very physical or not, there is no advantage (even participants that have permanent physical challenges are able to contribute equally), and working with food to create a meal can be physical enough to assist transformation. It has a very important end result, the creation of a meal for all

Get my personal help - See page 100 for details!

participants to partake, an important passive transformational opportunity. Perfectly suited to apply all of the TAC™ steps for team transformation. Also this program can be done indoors or outdoors so it's not weather dependent and sometimes can work very well with hotels and conference centers. In the right hands, can be done well for both large and small groups.

Cons- Be very wary of who conducts your program, many have no knowledge or experience in the team transformational realm, just the cooking background. A good way to guess if they are the right company for your team's transformation, research what they do. If they are a catering company, cooking school, culinary school or kitchen equipment retail sales company, run, don't walk the opposite directions. Unfortunately the saying, if it looks like a rose, it must be a rose does not apply in this case. Take a good whiff of this "rose" and if it doesn't smell like the real transformational experience that it can be, it probably smells of old fish!

Music & Rhythm Programs:

Pros- Also one of the programs that transcend cultural barriers and also in the right hands can be a very powerful transformational experience for your team if they follow the TAC™ steps of team transformation. If the program is conducted well, a final outcome could be recorded and used as a powerful auditory trigger much like the example used in the auditory trigger previous chapter. This program can be done indoors or outdoors depending on the acoustics and needs of the group. They can work very well at meeting sites like hotels and conference centers. Also works well with both large and small groups.

Cons- The final outcome produced by the team doesn't cover all of the senses and appeals more to auditory people. So the impact on the whole team is less than, say culinary which covers all of the senses.

Mystery Theatre:

Pros- At best, a fun team outing that works best between major team transformational programs that are mandatory. Adequate if the particular theatric group is very inclusive to include the whole team.

Cons- Not a viable option in transformation of a team.

Motivational Speaking:

Pros- Depends on the speaker and the process used. More applicable if used as a workshop not just a keynote because of the time needed for transformation. It is possible that the TAC™ steps for team transformation be applied. Usually a speaker with a background in NLP (neuro-linquistic programing) or hypnotherapy could accomplish transforming your team. Able to work with small or large groups and can go where ever your team meets, hotels, conference centers and meeting rooms.

Get my personal help - See page 100 for details!

Cons- Many speakers don't have a transformational plan, it's about selling their back of the room products, so make sure your speaker gets really clear to your needs and wants. Also, many speakers only speak; they don't conduct enough interaction exercise to make the experience rich enough for your team's transformation.

Indoor Team Games:

Pros- The games can be structured to focus on a particular team challenge. Look for a competent training company that uses the TAC™ steps for you team transformation. The programs can work with small or large groups and work well in ballrooms and conference rooms in hotels and conference centers.

Cons-Some games are so singularly focused that there is no pattern interrupt, an important part of TAC™. Also, some of the games do not have an interesting or compelling outcome that would not work well with certain personalities that need a compelling, non-contrived outcome.

Outdoor Team Games:

Pros- If these are the same as the indoor games, just done outside, then use the pros and cons from above. Usually outdoor games refer to the more physical team games that can only work outdoors and are usually geared for large groups. Many times they will refer to them as team Olympics, indicating a wide selection of games. They can be a very fun, afternoon in the park to get away from the office.

Get my personal help - See page 100 for details!

Cons- Make sure you bring along a First Aid kit and update your insurance to cover minor medical emergencies. Because these games focus is on physical activity, you are immediately segregating the physical people from the non-physical. And the people who are not physical but think they are will be the ones who really get physically injured and nothing puts a damper on a team experience than to have your department's manager carted away in an ambulance! This is not the right experience for transformation even if you team is very physical. Have you team go through transformation through one of the other suggested programs then enjoy a softball/picnic outing at the park as a great team shared experience.

Teamwork: Recipe to Your Business Success

Chapter Six:

How Do I Get Started?

Chapter Six:

How Do I Get Started?

What we need to do is learn to work in the system, by which I mean that everybody, every team, every platform, every division, every component is there not for individual competitive profit or recognition, but for contribution to the system as a whole on a win-win basis.
-W. Edward Deming

The hard part has already been done, knowing the steps towards your team's transformation as a new state of being. You've got a good idea of which of the six team characteristics that you'd like to focus. You've also have the awareness of what pitfalls have your team fell prey to or more likely will succumb to if something is not acted upon now. You also understand that your team's behavior is not who they are, but just a symptom of a challenge that your team has experienced from the past and it's being manifested now. You are also aware that not every team transformation process is created equally and that they must have all of the team transformation steps provided in the TAC™ (Team Associative Conditioning) process to make a profound effect and that your goal is to not change your team but to transform your team to a new state of being that brings you, your organization, your team, your company all of the rewards from the benefit of team synergy.

So how to get started?

Get my personal help - See page 100 for details!

Here are the steps to help you proceed with the confidence of knowing what is your outcome:

Step 1- Determine what is your outcome for your team. Yes, it's important to know what area of the six characteristics of a team you'd like to focus or suggest to your training company to focus. But this is a little different, write down what you'd like as an outcome for your team. What kind of transformational experience they would have, what kind of results from this transformation, what kind of behavior being demonstrated that influences other people, like co-workers, vendors and of course clients.

Step 2- Who are the people in your team? What is the make-up of the people, ages, gender, and cultural background? What job do they perform, are they all engineers, salespersons, executive level, mid-management, office workforce? What activities do they enjoy outside of the workplace, are the activities very physical, moderately physical, cerebral, playful, interactive or a mixture of all?

Step 3- Set a date(s) for team transformation or at least a proposed date. Even if you have to change the date because of schedule conflicts, by setting a date, you have now committed to your team and the transformation process would have begun.

Step 4- Contact the training company. If you have a company that has successfully transformed teams for you in the past and uses the TAC™ steps to accomplish this, then use them again. If finding the right company is new for you, here are some suggestions:

Ask around for referrals from within your company, from other companies like yours, from your HR department, from other vendors.

Use the list of types of team programs in Chapter 5 to determine what kind of program would work best for your team and the personality make-up of your team.

Google and other quality search engines of that type can be a good source of information in your search. Of course, by using Chapter 5 as a guideline, you can narrow your search.
If your team transformation experience is being held in conjunction with a meeting or conference, sometimes the host hotel or conference center can make suggestions of companies that they have had success working with on site.
Talk to someone at your local ASTD organization or speaker's bureau or call our company for a referral, call toll free 888-308-TEAM or (8326) or visit our web site www.ceochef.com .

The most important thing to remember, match your team's personality and needs to the program and make sure they have a TAC™ process to ensure success.

Step 5- Call the training company. Pick two to three companies to call and get bids. To ensure that you have found a possible candidate to train with your team, here are a couple of hints to let you know you've found a credible company.

Once you have found the right person in the training company to talk to, either an actual trainer, salesperson or customer service, make sure within your first conversation that they ask you, "what are your outcomes for your team?" This question should be repeated closer to the program to get a better bead on the outcomes, but if your possible training company does not ask that question up front, keep on moving to a company that does.

"Who are the people in your team, what do they do for you, what is their relationship with you, who are they?" should be the second question they ask you.

If they have asked you those questions, then proceed with giving them more information.

They will need the date or approximate date, the amount of time that is scheduled for the group (be aware, be flexible with the time, the most important thing is transformation), where it's being held (if you have not gotten that far in your planning, sometimes the training company can make suggestions on places they prefer).

If you've done other training programs with this group or another and what did you like or not like about the program. This will help the training company get very clear to how to structure your team experience.

Get my personal help - See page 100 for details!

Now you can ask for a beginning quote to be sent to you. They may be able to give you a verbal quote of their program, but it's always best to get a beginning quote that includes the basic information that you've given to them already. So you know what is included within that quote and what is not included.

Some things to consider when getting a price quote:

Even though everyone wants to get the best deal possible, remember, you are basing the future performance of your team on the quality of training. This is not like buying a car for basic transportation. A luxury car or a standard sedan will get you from point A to point B. This is the state of being of your team which can make or break your company, department, or division. What is the success of those things worth to you? If this team is responsible for a project that could catapult your business to the next level or is this the team that helps determine the direction of your small business, what is that worth to you?

Choose the right training company that will get you the results you must have for the health and success of your company, period!

Step 6-If the choice is not clear to which company is best for you, conduct a conference call with a close colleagues and/or person from HR to interview the potential training companies. Use the TAC™ guidelines to help you determine if they are the right ones for the job.

Step 7- Finalize your logistics, time, dates, and location and ask for a final proposal contract from the company that you have chosen. Most companies will have you pay some kind of deposit to hold the date, usually at least 50% of the training quote and an estimate of travel expenses, also paid up front. Some training companies will offer reward pricing if your program is paid in full a date before the program. Some times this can be as much as 5% of the total price.

Remember, good training companies will hold a date for only so long and the sooner you commit to them with a signed contract and deposit, the more time they can devote on focusing on your team's program.

Step 8- If the training company has not scheduled one more meeting about your training day, then you need to schedule a day. Usually a week or two before the program is best to talk. Your circumstances within teams change, new personnel, changing challenges, new projects; so the freshest, most current information would serve your training company and team best to be applied to your program.

Note about travel:
If the training company that you choose is from outside the area, there will be travel expenses involved in getting a trainer(s) to your training site. Most trainers will go anywhere to do what they do best; they are passionate and committed in what they do for you and your team. They will be most effective if they have the least amount of travel

Get my personal help - See page 100 for details!

stress so they are fresh and ready for your team. This is not the time to get cheap and insist on certain flights, rental car restrictions, per diem caps, etc... Most training companies are respectful that you are picking up the tab for travel, but if there is an opportunity for an air travel upgrade, or better flight time, let them have it, your team and the results for your team, will benefit greatly.

Chapter Seven:

Final Team Thoughts

Chapter Seven:

Final Team Thoughts

Even if you are on the right track, you'll get run over if you just sit there.
-Will Rogers

If you have completed this book, congratulations! You are first among a growing trend to build solid teams within and around our organization. You have the intellect to understand that the key to any business, small business or organization success is highly motivated, skilled, world class teams that become your biggest asset to finding the results that you deserve.

Now is the time to take action. To create real synergy within your organization you must create a sense of urgency, an attitude of "now" is the time to take action in every area of your organization. Whether you're a large corporation, with many divisions and departments, or a small business with an outside virtual team, and in between, now is the time to take your teams to the next level. Like the book title, "Good to Great", every team needs to reassert themselves, re-commit themselves, and basically transform themselves to compete in a new world economy.

Take the next step and invest in your most powerful asset that you could ever have, your teams!

Get my personal help - See page 100 for details!

More Quotes

From other notable people who value the power of team! From industry...

Coming together is a beginning,
Keeping together is progress,
Working together is success.
-Henry Ford

From the world of sports...

Talent wins games, but teamwork and intelligence wins championships.
-Michael Jordan

One man can be a crucial ingredient on a team, but one man cannot make a team.
-Kareem Abdul-Jabbar

From spiritual leaders...

None of us, including me, ever do great things. But we can all do small things, with great love, and together we can do something wonderful.
-Mother Teresa

From Greek epic poets...

Light is the task where many share the toil.
-Homer

Get my personal help - See page 100 for details!

Products & Services:

To learn more about our interactive, highly effective team building workshops and ask for,
Corporate Culinary Challenge™
Visit our web site, www.ceochef.com or
Call our toll free number: 888-308-TEAM (8326)

To learn more about having Chef Jim speak at your next conference or meeting, visit www.ceochef.com or
Call our toll free number: 888-308-8326

To inquire about the latest books, CD's, DVD's and other transformation tools to support your teams and leaders, email us at info@ceochef.com and we'll send you the latest updates to our team and leadership tools.

Other services to ask about:

- ✓ Team Coaching
- ✓ Team Tele-Coaching
- ✓ Celebrity Appearances
- ✓ Team & Leadership Retreats
- ✓ Team Building
- ✓ Keynote Speech

FREE Stuff!

"You are the average of the five people you spend the most time with"
-Jim Rohn

It's not easy to stay "in" the change.
And with all of us, being bomb-barded by the media with messages that don't support our new team mindset, we need support.

I invite you to be a part of our Kitchen Brigade (a fancy term for team!) and stay connected to the continuing message of empowerment, creativity, productivity and fun!

Send us an email to join at info@ceochef.com or call us, toll free at: 888-308-TEAM (8326) or go to our website www.ceochef.com .

Of course, membership has its privileges:
- ✓ FREE - e-report- "6 Mistakes That Guarantee Dysfunctional Teams in Your Workplace"
- ✓ FREE - 90 Days to Amazing Kitchen Results!
- ✓ FREE - updates to "Kitchen Wisdom" latest blog of team inspiration, information, recipes, cooking secrets
- ✓ Monthly Newsletter
- ✓ FREE - updates of first-hand information on Chef Jim's next celebrity appearance in your area.
- ✓ And much much more...

Quick Order Form

Fax orders: 888-308-8326

Telephone Orders: Call 888-308-TEAM (8326) and have your credit card ready.

Email orders: orders@ceochef.com

Postal Orders: CEO Chef, Jim Connolly,

311 N. Robertson Blvd. #888, Beverly Hills, CA 90211

818-407-8883

Prices:

1-10	15.95 each
11-50	12.95 each
50-100	10.95 each

More than 100 - call for quote

Add $4.95 shipping for the first book, $2.00 every other book

Name _____

Shipping Address _____

_____

Credit Card# _____

Exp. Date_____ Card Type _____

Billing Address (if different)

_____

_____

We accept Visa, Master Card, AMEX and Discovery!

www.ingramcontent.com/pod-product-compliance
Lightning Source LLC
Chambersburg PA
CBHW051339170526
45166CB00002B/874